Machine Learning with Scikit-Learn and
TensorFlow

Deep Learning with Python (Random Forests, Decision Trees, and Neural Networks)

By Emery H. Maxwell

Disclaimer:

The views expressed within this book are those of the author alone. All copyrights and trademarks are properties of their respective owners. The information contained within this book is based on the opinions, observations, and experiences of the author and is provided "AS-IS". No warranties of any kind are made. Neither the author nor publisher are engaged in rendering professional services of any kind. Neither the author nor publisher will assume responsibility or liability for any loss or damage related directly or indirectly to the information contained within this book.

The author has attempted to be as accurate as possible with the information contained within this book. Neither the author nor publisher will assume responsibility or liability for any errors, omissions, inconsistencies, or inaccuracies.

Table of Contents

Introduction

Welcome to the *Machine Learning with Scikit-Learn and TensorFlow* guide. This book is intended to help you understand and apply neural networks and machine learning concepts with Decision Trees, Random Forests, Scikit-Learn, TensorFlow, and Python.

It appears that the development of artificial intelligence is expanding. Certain tools are working behind the scenes of everyday life as prediction models by allowing computers to learn and act without human intervention.

The result so far has been self-driving vehicles, improved internet browsing, and more.

Consider algorithms.

Many of the online businesses you see on the web today are driven by algorithms, which are used to predict what the person would like to search for. Essentially, they are implementing it as a marketing strategy, which can make things more efficient for the buyer and seller.

In computer science and mathematics, an algorithm is a method of how to solve problems. It acts as a step-by-step set of mathematical guidelines that explain how to perform a certain task.

When you browse the web, the advertisements that pop up are often catered to your interests through the use of algorithmic programming.

For example, watching a stock market video on social media can bring up advertisements on your computer that are related to the stock market.

The auto-suggest feature on search engines is also based on algorithmic programming. They are programmed to fill in the blanks and predict what you are going to type next.

This explains why the gaps are often filled in for you in the search box.

For example, if users enter How to B in the search box, it might look something like this:

How to B

How to b**ake a cake**

How to b**e more productive**

How to b**e more confident**

How to b**ecome an electrician**

How to b**e an explorer**

How to b**e happier**

How to b**uild a house**

How to b**uild a canoe for beginners**

How to b**uy a house**

How to b**uy your first car**

But many people don't understand how an algorithm like this works, nor do they understand the programming language that drives it.

Even if you are not a programmer or data scientist, it can still be interesting to discover how machine learning works.

Python's simplistic language makes it ideal for beginners to use for automation, network programming, web apps, data mining, and more. It works on various platforms, including *Windows, Linux, Mac.*

This book is intended to guide you through the fundamentals of machine learning through *Python, Scikit-Learn,* and *TensorFlow.*

It will cover:

- **An overview of *Python*, neural networks, *Scikit-Learn*, *TensorFlow*, random forests, decision trees, machine learning, and deep learning**

- **How to get started with *Python***

- **How to run a line of code**

- **How to get started with *Scikit-Learn***

- **How to work with data**

- **How to use *TensorFlow***

- **How to use datasets**

- **Computational graphs**

- **How search algorithms work**

- **How clustering algorithms work**

- **. . . and more**

Overview

T his section will include an overview of *Python, Neural Networks, Scikit-Learn, TensorFlow, Random Forests, Decision Trees, Machine Learning,* and *Deep Learning.*

The purpose is to provide a basic understanding of these terms and their functions before delving any further.

Overview of Python

Python is a general-purpose programming language that has an emphasis on code readability, using significant whitespace. Its emphasis on readability reduces the cost of program maintenance.

Since it has built-in data structures that are high-level, rapid application development is made possible. It also has the ability to connect existing components together.

Python is open source and can be freely distributed.

It has a standard comprehensive library, and interpreters are available for a variety of operating systems.

Overview of Neural Networks

Neural networks are decision making tools, and although they require a large variety of training for real-world operation, they are one of the most useful forms of artificial intelligence.

Essentially, they are interconnected groups of natural or artificial neurons that use a mathematical or computation model for the processing of information, like a computerized brain.

Neural networks can be used for the purposes of finding patterns in data. Learning in neural networks is quite useful in applications where the task is so complex that it becomes manually impractical.

Overview of Scikit-learn

Scikit-learn is a free, open source machine learning library for *Python*. It features simple tools for data mining and data analysis.

Built on the scientific *Python* libraries of *NumPy* and *Scipy*, *Scikit-leqrn* is reusable in various contexts.

It helps identify to which category an object belongs to, predict a continuous-valued attribute associated with an object, and automatically groups similar objects into sets.

TensorFlow

Tensorflow is a free and open source machine learning software library for dataflow and differentiable programming, and it is used for machine learning applications. Essentially, it is a math library, so to speak.

It offers *Python* and *C APIs*. Without *API* backwards compatibility, it also provides *Java, JavaScript, Go Java, Swift,* and *C++*. Additionally, it supports various add-on libraries, including *TensorFlowProbability, Tensor2Tensor, Ragged Tensors,* and *BERT*.

Random Forests

Random forests are a type of learning method in which multiple learning algorithms are used to obtain improved predictive performance. They are used for classification, regression, and other tasks.

They operate by the construction of many decision trees and outputting the class that is the mode of the classes or mean prediction of the individual trees.

They are intended to improve the ways that technologies analyze complex data.

Decision Trees

Decision trees are tree-like graphs that illustrate a variety of possible outcomes of a decision. Branches are used to represent different choices and their risks, costs, etc.

To illustrate:

Does the client have at least $100,000 worth of assets?

Age < 40

Yes? No?

Had a   Saved at least 30%

high-paying career for   of your annual income

at least the past seven years?   for at least fifteen years?

Yes? No?   Yes? No?

>$100,000 <$100,000 >$100,000 <$100,000

Machine Learning

Machine learning is a branch of artificial intelligence that gives computers the ability to perform a task without having to rely on human instructions.

Instead of dealing with direct instructions from humans, they rely on patterns instead, building data to make predictions or decisions.

When people do a certain thing for long enough, they might eventually develop a feel for it. An experienced investor might develop a feel for a profitable stock to invest in, knowing how to identify low-risk/high-reward situations in the market. Similarly, machine learning attempts to give this same type of ability to computers.

Machine learning tasks consist of:

• **Supervised learning-** this is where the algorithm builds a mathematical model in which the inputs and outputs are both present. In this case, a full set of labeled data is available.

*Having a full set of labels is when the examples in the training set of data is labeled with the solution the algorithm is supposed to generate on its own.

To illustrate, picture a business that is expanding and hiring more personnel to keep up with the increased demands. An issue arises because the business owner's new and inexperienced staff doesn't yet know how to effectively run the business when the owner is away.

The owner decides to create an app that can estimate the costs for the products that the company produces. To create the app, he jots down the costs for production, shipping, and handling on the products that his company currently sells. Then he feeds the full set of training data about each product into his machine learning algorithm.

After the app shows the staff what the costs for the production, shipping, and handling of the products are, they can then determine their pricing strategy for any similar products the company creates in the near future.

• **Semi-supervised learning-** In this model, the algorithm develops a mathematical model from data that is incomplete and a part of the sample input is unlabeled.

• **Unsupervised learning-** this is where the algorithm builds a mathematical model in which only the inputs are present. In this case, the model is given a set of data without explicit instructions.

To illustrate, let's say the business owner does *not* have access to the pricing information for his products. But since he *does* have access to the size, weight, and general nature of the products, the algorithm can work with that information.

In this case, the algorithm might be able to use this data to identify the median price a customer would pay for a product of similar nature.

Deep Learning

Deep learning is essentially a series of algorithms used in machine learning. Since the input runs deeper than many machine learning algorithms, *Deep learning* can be considered more extreme than machine learning.

It relies on whichever training process it has to work with in order to find useful patterns in the examples, instead of relying on the manual identification of features.

Generally, basic machine learning algorithms are assembled in graphs with straight lines, but deep learning algorithms are assembled in groups that are ranked by importance.

How to Get Started with Python

If you haven't done so yet, check to see if you have *Python* installed on your computer, as some systems come with it already installed.

To check if it's already installed on your computer, type **python** into the start bar window and see what pops up.

You can also enter the text **cmd.exe** into the start bar, and then click on the icon that comes up. From there, you should get a screen that looks like this: C:\Users*Computer User Name*>

From that screen, enter the text: **python --version** after the arrow, so it will then look like this: C:\Users*Computer User Name*>python --version. Then hit **Enter** on the keyboard.

Downloading and Installing Python

If you don't already have it, you can download the latest version of *Python* for free by going to https://www.python.org/downloads/

Tip: In order to do *Python* Programming, you will need an interpreter. An interpreter is simply a computer program that executes program instructions by interpreting a high-level programming code into code that can be understood by the machine. The interpreter can be downloaded at https://thonny.org/

Putting codes into *Python* scripts saves you from having to reenter everything each time you want to change it.

If you already have *Python*, but you're unsure if you are running the latest one, you can check which version you are currently running by opening the terminal and running this command:

Shell

python -v

Tip for *Windows* users: During the *Python* download and installation process, when you reach the **Customize *Python*** screen, make sure the **Add python.exe to Path** option is selected.

Python Installation Confirmation

To ensure that *Python* did indeed install effectively, open the *Python Interactive Shell*.

• *Windows*: After opening the terminal, run: *python* or *py -3*, depending on which one you have.

• *Linux:* After opening the terminal, run: *python*.

• *Mac*: After opening the terminal, run: *python* or *python3*, depending on which one you have.

Tip for *Windows* Users: To check if your account has administrative privileges:

1.) Right-click the command prompt icon.

2.) Select **Run as Administrator**.

By now, the **Python Shell** should open.

How to Run a Line of Code

With the command prompt window open, you can begin to experiment with running a line of code. The command prompt window is the one with the black screen that should have some general *Python* information on it, including the version, date of inception, etc.

Underneath the wording that says: *Type "help", "copyright", "credits" or "license" for more information*, there should be three arrows. The right side of the arrows is where you type the codes.

In *Python 2*, using parenthesis inside the code are not necessary to be able to print something, but they must be used in *Python 3*.

1.) Start out by typing the word *print*.

2.) Using quotation marks, type what you want to write, using parenthesis if you're using *Python 3*.

3.) Press **Enter** on the keyboard.

For example, in *python 2*, it might look something like this:

>>> print "Hello World!"

In *python 3*, it should look like this:

>>> print ("Hello World!")

If done correctly, after hitting the **Enter** key, the text should look like this:

Hello World!

That's just about it. Continue to experiment with entering lines and having *Python* execute the statement.

How to Get Started with Scikit-Learn

In order to use *Scikit-Learn*, you need to already have *Python* *(2.7 or newer, or 3.4 or newer)*, *Numpy (1.8.2 or newer)*, and *SciPy (0.13.3 or newer)* libraries installed.

Note: *Scikit-learn* 0.20 is the last version that supports *Python 2.7 and Python 3.4*. *Scikit-learn* 0.21 requires a version of *Python 3.5 or* newer.

Here are some of the algorithms it features:

• **Classification**

• **Regression**

• **Clustering**

How to Install Scikit-Learn

The installation of *Scikit-Learn,* as well as the installation of *Numpy* and *Scipy,*can be achieved by using *Conda* or *pip.*

Pip and *Conda* are both package (library) management systems.

Pip is a tool that automatically comes with *Python*. But *Conda* can install *Python Programming Language*, while *pip* cannot.

If you already have a functioning version of *Numpy* and Scipy, and would like to install *Scikit-learn* by using *pip*, open the terminal of your operating system and run this command:

pip install -U scikit-learn

To install *Scikit-learn* by using *Conda*, open the terminal of your operating system and run this command:

conda install scikit-learn

Once the installation is complete, *Scikit-Learn* can be imported into *Python*. This is a necessary step in order to use its algorithms. To import it, use the following statement:

import sklearn

Even if you do not have *Scipy* and *Numpy* yet, they can also be installed via *pip*.

Note: When using *pip*, try to make sure that *Numpy* and *Scipy* are not recompiled from source, and *binary wheels* are used. This can save you the trouble of making things more complex than necessary, as building *Numpy* and *Scipy* from source requires careful configuration.

To install *Scikit-learn* along with its dependencies via *pip*, install it as:

scikit-learn [alldeps]

To upgrade *Scikit-learn* installed via *Anaconda* (*Conda*), use the command:

conda update scikit-learn

To uninstall *Scikit-learn* that had been installed via *Conda*, use the command:

conda remove scikit-learn

Problem Settings

Learning problems are grouped into the categories of supervised learning, unsupervised learning, classification, and regression.

• **Classification**: this is the process of categorizing data into a variety of classes. A situation in which one has a limited number of categories and for every *n* sample provided, one would try to label them with the correct class.

An example would be a situation that involved a series of two different classes of labels. One class is *W*, and the other class is *R*. The *R*'s are sitting on a graph with the points reading 0 through 2, while the *W*'s are on the same graph with the points reading 3 through 5.

In this case, a classification algorithm can be used for the purpose of drawing a dividing line between the two clusters of points to separate them. The line now allows the generalization of new data, so if you placed another point onto the graph, the algorithm would be able to predict whether it's a *R* point or *W* point.

5- WWWW

4- WWWW

3- WWWW

————————

2-RRRRR

1-RRRRR

0- RRRRR

0- 1- 2- 3- 4- 5-

Regression: this is when the desired output includes one or more continuous variables. Essentially, it's when the model is given a y value to predict the x value. For example, the prediction of the length of a flower based off its age and weight.

Understanding the behavior of the stock market through the use of tools would be a form of regression.

If you were to build a Stock trading algorithm, you would likely want to include a variety of variables in the dataset. These variables would likely include the date, opening price, previous day's closing price, number of shares being traded, high of the day, low of the day, moving averages, etc.

Such an algorithm would work by using those variables to predict where the stock may be heading. The person building the algorithm would break the process down into steps, and then combine them all at the end to get a functioning prediction tool.

The first step could be the creation of a dataframe that contains just the date and closing price. The next step might include the number of shares being traded, and so on.

If implemented correctly, the result would be that the trader would no longer need to monitor live prices on the charts or manually place buy and sell orders. There would also be the added benefit of not having to make trading decisions based on human emotions such as fear and greed.

Once completed, these algorithms are often tested out by monitoring how they perform with real stock market data from the past. It is crucial to ensure that the historical data being tested has a sufficient number of data points, so a sufficient number of sample trades can take place, having them test different scenarios.

For an overview of **supervised learning** and **unsupervised learning**, refer to the *Machine Learning* subsection in the *Overview* chapter.

Working with Data in Scikit-Learn

$\mathbf{M}$achine learning algorithms used in *scikit-learn* work with data that is in a *two-dimensional array* or *matrix*. The size of the array is supposed to be [n_samples, n_features]

• **n_samples**: the number of samples. A sample might be a video, sound, picture, or a document.

• **n_features**: the number of features (traits) for each sample.

A learning problem will generally consider a set of *n* data samples and then try to predict the properties of unknown data. When every sample is greater than a single number, it is known to have a variety of features.

To import datasets from the *Scikit-learn* library, use the code:

from sklearn import datasets

Then load the dataset you would like to display.

For example, if you would like to load the *iris* dataset that comes with the *Scikit-learn* data science library, use the commands:

from sklearn import datasets

iris = datasets.load_iris ()

There are various commands that can be used to obtain the characteristics of datasets.

For example, to obtain information for the *Iris Flower* dataset, use the command:

print (iris.data)

To obtain information on the various labels of the flowers, use the command:

print (iris.target)

To obtain an array of label names in the flower dataset, use the command:

print (iris.target_names)

Toy Datasets

There are some standard datasets that come along with *scikit-learn*, so you don't have to download the file from another website.

Although they are often too small to represent real world machine learning tasks, they can be useful to rapidly illustrate the behavior of the different algorithms used in *scikit-learn*.

To load them, use these functions:

load_boston ([return_X_y])

Load and return the Boston house prices dataset (regression).

load_iris ([return_X_y])

Load and return the iris dataset (classification).

load_diabetes ([return_X_y])

Load and return the diabetes dataset (regression).

load_breast_cancer ([return_X_y])

Load and return the breast cancer Wisconsin dataset (classification).

load_wine ([return_X_y])

Load and return the wine dataset (classification).

load_linnerud ([return_X_y])

Load and return the linnerud dataset (multivariate regression).

load_digits ([n_class, return_X_y])

Load and return the digits dataset (classification).

Real World Datasets

Scikit-learn also has tools to load bigger datasets.

To load them, use these functions:

fetch_california_housing ([data_home, …])

Load the California housing dataset (regression).

fetch_kddcup99 ([subset, data_home, shuffle, ...])

Load the kddcup99 dataset (classification).

fetch_rcv1 ([data_home, subset, ...])

Load the RCV1 multilabel dataset (classification).

fetch_covtype ([data_home, ...])

Load the covertype dataset (classification)

fetch_lfw_pairs ([subset, data_home, ...])

Load the *Labeled Faces in the Wild* (LFW) pairs dataset (classification).

fetch_lfw_people ([data_home, funneled, ...])

Load the *Labeled Faces in the Wild* (LFW) people dataset (classification).

fetch_20newsgroups_vectorized ([subset, ...])

Load the 20 newsgroups dataset and vectorize it into token counts (classification).

fetch_olivetti_faces ([data_home, shuffle, …])

Load the *Olivetti* faces dataset from AT&T (classification)

Downloading Datasets

Datasets can also be downloaded via https://www.openml.org/, which is a public repository for machine learning data and experiments. It is available to anyone who would like to upload open datasets.

The *sklearn.datasets* package is capable of downloading datasets from that repository by using the following function:

sklearn.datasets.fetch_openml

Here is an example of downloading a dataset of gene expressions in mice brains:

```
>>> from sklearn.datasets import fetch_openml

>>> mice = fetch_openml (name= 'miceprotein', version=4)
```

Neural Network Models

Neural networks exist to mimic the thinking processes of a human brain. They are a type of deep learning algorithm that specialize in feature selection.

A neural network typically consists of dozens to millions of artificial neurons (units). These units are arranged in a series of layers that connect to each other.

These units can be:

• **input units-** these units are programmed to receive different forms of information from the external world.

• **output units-** these units signal how the network responds to the information it has learned.

• **hidden units-**these units are in between the input and output units. They serve as a sort of middle ground.

Utilizing these inputs, a neural network learns by remembering what went wrong earlier, and then modifying itself to do better by comparing the outcomes of what *actually* transpired and what was *supposed* to transpire. The output that the network produced is compared with the result that it was *supposed* to produce.

This process is known as ***Backpropagation***.

The sklearn.neural_network module has models that are based on neural networks.

neural_network.BernoulliRBM ([components, ...])

Bermoulli Restricted Boltzman Machine (RBM).

neural_network.MLPClassifier ([...])

Multi-layer Perception classifier.

neural_network.MLPRegressor([...])

Multi-layer Perception regressor.

Decision Trees with Scikit-Learn

T he purpose of decision trees is to create a workable model that is able to predict the value of a target variable by learning from data features.

A decision tree is a tool that uses a model of decisions to help identify a strategy that is most probable to solve a problem.

Since decision trees only have splitting paths and no converging paths, they can grow quite large when used manually.

Scikit-learn uses the Classification and Regression Trees (CART) algorithm.

Scikit-learn has a module called **sklearn.tree**, which has decision tree-based models for classification and regression.

tree.DecisionTreeClassifier ([criterion, …])

Decision tree classifier.

tree.DecisionTreeRegressor ([criterion, …])

Decision tree regressor.

tree.ExtraTreeClassifier ([criterion, …])

Highly randomized tree classifier.

tree.ExtraTreeRegressor ([criterion, …])

Highly randomized tree regressor.

tree.export_graphviz (decision_tree[, …])

Export a decision tree in DOT format.

If you were to use the *Iris* dataset, to construct a decision tree, it can be done by using this series of commands:

```
>>> from sklearn.datasets import load_iris
>>> from sklearn import tree
>>> iris = load_iris ()
>>> clf = tree.DecisionTreeClassifier ()
>>> clf = clf.fit (iris.data, iris.target)
```

After the tree has been trained, it can be plotted with this command:

```
>>> tree.plot_tree(clf.fit(iris.data, iris.target))
```

TensorFlow

Machine learning models can also be built with *TensorFlow*. This machine learning framework is based on data graphs, and it can definitely come in handy if you are interested in neural networks and deep learning. It uses *Python* to provide an API for building applications with the framework.

There is even a version (*TensorFlow Lite*) for smaller devices, so you can obtain machine learning on your phone.

To explain how *TensorFlow* works, it definitely helps to understand what its moving parts (tensors and nodes) are.

Tensors: arrays of numbers or functions.

Each tensor consists of:

• a shape

• a name

• a data type

The different types of tensors that can be created are as follows:

• tf.Variable

• tf.placeholder

• tf.constant

• tf.Sparsetensor

Node: a point of connection within a network.

To illustrate, if there was a 3x3 matrix with numerical values of 1 through 9, *TensorFlow* might represent it as something like this:

[[1, 2, 3],

[4, 5, 6],

[7, 8, 9]]

In *TensorFlow*, everything is based on the creation of a computational graph.

Generally, the computational graph is a network of nodes. Each node is essentially an operation that runs a function. The function can be something simple or complex. Each operation can generate a certain amount (including zero) of tensors which can be used in the graph.

In *TensorFlow*, the tensors flow through the graph and connect the nodes.

Although the math operations are not done by *Python*, it serves as a traffic director between *TensorFlow* and the C++ binaries that the libraries are written as. In other words, the libraries of transformations are written in C++, and *Python* connects that to *TensorFlow*.

Automatic Differentiation is included in the *TensorFlow* framework, and it serves to calculate derivatives from the computation graph automatically. This can be helpful because it saves the user from having to manually type in a code each time in order to àssemble a new arrangement of neural networks.

The nodes have gradient operations attached to them. These gradient operations calculate the derivatives of input in regards to output. Next, the gradients in regards to parameters are calculated during the process of backpropagation.

For a reminder on how **Backpropagation** works, refer to the *Neural Network Models* section in the *Working with Data in Scikit-Learn* chapter.

How to Install TensorFlow

For *Windows* users, *TensorFlow* can be installed with *pip*, the package (library) management system that comes with *Python*.

Note: Installing *TensorFlow* with *pip* might cause interference issues with other *Python* installations on your operating system, as it will override existing libraries and install specific versions in order to comply with dependencies.

To install *TensorFlow* on CPU with *pip*, use the command:

pip install tensorflow

Since *Python3* comes with *pip3*, that program can be used to install *TensorFlow*.

To install the CPU-only version for *TensorFlow,* use the command:

pip3 install –upgrade tensorflow

To install the GPU version for *TensorFlow*, use the command:

pip3 install –upgrade tensorflow-gpu

To install *TensorFlow 2.0 Alpha*, use the command:

pip install tensorflow==2.0.0-alpha0

Importing *TensoFlow* as tf for short will save keystrokes later on, since your machine will allow you to refer to *TensorFlow* as *tf*. But you can name it anything you like.

To import *TensorFlow* as tf, use the command:

Import tensorflow as tf

If you have *numpy*, you might also want to import that by a code name for short:

import numpy as np

To check that you have the correct version running on your system, use the commands:

import tensorflow as tf

print (tf._version_)

The output should tell you the version you have running on your system.

How to Install Jupyter

If you'd like to install *Jupyter*, the notebook viewer that allows you to write codes and rich text elements, you must first activate the *tensorflow* environment. To do that, use the commands:

For Windows Users

activate tensorflow

pip install matplotlib jupyter

For Linux and Mac

source activate tensorflow

pip install matplotlib jupyter

How to Use Datasets

To import datasets

```
import tensorflow_datasets as tfds
```

Fetch the DatasetBuilder class by string

```
mnist_builder = tfds.builder("mnist)
```

Download the dataset

```
mnist_builder.download_and_prepare()
```

Construct the tf.data.Dataset

```
ds = mnist_builder.as_dataset(split=tfds.Split.TRAIN)
```

Obtain information for the dataset

```
info = mnist_builder.info
print(info)
```

Computational Graphs

Since *TensorFlow* is based on graph computation, it can help to take a look at an example of a computational graph to gain an even better understanding of how the framework operates.

Let's say **a=(b+c) *(c+5)**.

This equation can be broken down into steps.

So now it could look like:

d= b+c

e= c+5

a= d*e

Now that the equation has been broken down into three steps, it can be placed onto a graph.

Here's what it might look like:

a=d*e

♂ ↑

d=b+c e=c+5

↑ ↑

b c

Notice how the series of nodes are connected to each other in the graph above, the arrows indicating their connection. In the graph, each node is essentially an operation (op). Each node takes a certain number of tensors as inputs and creates a tensor as an output.

TensorFlow works through the use of graph building and session running. After the graph of data gets built, a session can be ran to execute the operations of the graph. From a technical standpoint, a session is a run-time environment that connects the hardware it is going to run in.

One of the good things about it is that the user does not have to run the entire graph in order for individual pieces to work. Individual parts of the graph can be controlled and executed separately, which advantageously gives the user flexibility with the data models.

Common Operations in TensorFlow

- **tf.add**

- **tf.subtract**

- **tf.multiply**

- **tf.div**

- **tf.exp**

- **tf.pow**

- **tf.sqrt**

These operations will need to be paired up with at least one variable in order for them to work.

To illustrate:

- **tf.add(a, b)**

- **tf.subtract(a, b)**

- **tf.multiply(a, b)**

- **tf.div(a,b)**

- **tf.exp(a)**

- **tf.pow(a, b)**

- **tf.sqrt(a)**

To illustrate:

 # Add

tensor_a = tf.constant([[1, 2]], dtype = tf.int32)

tensor_b = tf.constant([[3, 4]], dtype = tf.int32)

tensor_add = tf.add(tensor_a, tensor_b)print(tensor_add)

Then the output would be:

Tensor("Add:0", shape=(1, 2), dtype=int32)

That example demonstrated two tensors being constructed, then added up. The first tensor had the numbers 1 and 2, and the other tensor had the numbers 3 and 4.

Algorithms

Algorithms play a fairly substantial role in machine learning. Operating on a set of rules or formulas that work together to solve a problem, they are capable of performing data processing, calculation, automated reasoning, and more. They are intended to produce an output from an input.

Algorithms Supported by TensorFlow

• Linear regression:

tf.estimator.LinearRegressor

• Classification:

tf.estimator.LinearClassifier

• Boosted tree classification:

tf.estimator.BoostedTreesClassifier

• Boosted tree regression:

tf.estimator.BoostedTreesRegressor

• Deep learning classification:

tf.estimator.DNNClassifier

Deep learning wipe and deep:

tf.estimator.DNNLinearCombinedClassifier

How Search Algorithms Work

Many factors come into play when a search algorithm is at work.

These factors include:

• Analysis

• Matching

• Ranking

• History

• Settings

• Location

• Results

Analysis

Even when a user misspells something, a search algorithm will "decode" what that person is searching for. This is accomplished through the use of indexing, which is a term used to describe the organization of data according to a particular plan. Indexing helps information appear more presentable.

Matching

In this step, the frequency in which the search criteria show up in relevant places, such as, the web page, images, or other content, is analyzed. The more popular the website, the more relevant it becomes to the search engine.

Ranking

Page ranking is all about bringing what the search algorithm considers to be the most relevant to the forefront of web traffic. Ranking is often determined by web site popularity. A web site that receives many visitors will usually outrank a web site with few visitors.

History

Previous search history is certainly a major factor to be taken into consideration when assessing search algorithms.

Browsing history can be tracked via the use of 1st and 3rd party cookies. Tracking cookies can follow people around the web. Tracking cookies are not welcomed by everyone, and many web sites have warnings displayed to let the visitor know that the site uses cookies.

Settings

Depending on what kind of settings a computer user has, a search algorithm may adapt itself to certain parameters in accordance to the person's preferences.

For example, enabling *Secure Search* in the *Settings* sectionmight prevent certain results from being displayed during a web browsing session.

Location

Different areas of the world can cause the algorithm to bring different search results.

For example, searching for the term, "government official" might bring back results on the President of the United States if the person was performing the search in America.

But the same search term, "government official" might bring back results referring to the Prime Minister of the United Kingdom if the person was performing the search from there. Or it might bring back search results for the Prime Minister of Canada if the search was being performed from Toronto, Ontario.

Results

This is where all the processed information comes together after it has been calculated. If a person doing search engine optimization finds terms that are in high demand but have fairly low supply, that person will stand a better chance at having his or her web site show up on the first or second page of the search results.

How Clustering Algorithms Work

When a set of data points are given, they can be grouped into clusters so that points within each cluster are alike and points from different clusters are unalike. That data points that are grouped together are referred to as clusters.

Clustering falls in the "unsupervised learning" category, and it is often used for statistical data analysis.

There are different types of clustering algorithms, including:

• **Agglomerative Hierarchical Clustering**

• **Gaussian Mixture Models**

• **Density-Based Spatial Clustering of Applications with Noise (DBSCAN)**

• **Mean-Shift Clustering**

• **K-means Clustering**

But since the K-means clustering algorithm is the easiest one to implement, this section will focus on that one.

They can be used to:

• Create profiles by monitoring activity

• Identify if a computer user is an actual person and not a robot. An example of this would be filling out information on a website and being asked how many of the images have signs in them (or a similar question).

• Categorize inventory based on sales history

• Customer Segmentation based on purchase history

• Cyber-profiling criminals by classifying the types of criminals who were present at the crime scene

• Image Segmentation

To illustrate a K-means Clustering algorithm:

Dog Breeds

German Shepherds

H H H H

H H H H

H H H H

Spaniels

HHH

HHH

HHH

Golden Retrievers

H H H

H H H

· H H H

Height

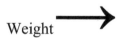

Weight

Notice the differences in the data classes in the above example. In this case, the differences were demonstrated through the use of spacing between the letter H. Using the letter H, German Shepherds had the widest gap between them to demonstrate that they are the largest, while Spaniels had the smallest gap to demonstrate that they are the smallest of the breeds in the example.

In this case, if the machine was trained correctly, and it was trying to figure out which breed a particular dog was, and it received information that read, H H H H, it would conclude that the breed is a German Shepherd.

The letter H demonstrated how the properties were alike, but the amount of spaces between demonstrates how they are *unalike*.

For a similar example, refer to the *Problem Settings* chapter.

To use K-means clustering with *Python*, the libraries must first be imported.

import pandas as pd

import numpy as np

import matplotlib.pyplot as plt

from sklearn.cluster import KMeans

%matplotlib inline

After the libraries have been imported, try to create some random data in a two-dimensional space to use as an example. The 0 can represent the "0 cluster" and the 1 can represent the "1 cluster." Using this method, the goal at the end would be to have a total of fifty zeros and fifty ones as a result.

x= -2 * np.random.rand (100 ,2)

x1 = 1 + 2 * np.random.rand (50, 2)

x [50:100, :] = x1

plt.scatter (x[: , 0], x[:, 1], s = 50, c = 'b')

plt.show ( )

In this example, one hundred data points were created and separated into two groups. Each group has fifty data points.

Then *Scikit-learn* can be used to process the data.

from sklearn.cluster import KMeans

Kmean = KMeans (n_clusters=2)

Kmean.fit (x)

Then the centroid can be found.

Kmean.cluster_centers_

Using the result, the cluster centroids can be displayed using the colors red and green.

plt.scatter (x [: , 0], x[: , 1], s =50, c='b')

plt.scatter (-0.94665068, -0.97138368, s=200, c='g', marker='s')

plt.scatter (2.01559419, 2.02597093, s=200, c='r', marker='s')

plt.show ( )

To test the algorithm, use the command:

Kmean.labels_

<u>Closing</u>

Although artificial intelligence may be advancing, there is no solid reason to believe it ever will or should entirely replace humans.

I believe machine learning should be used to help humans; not replace them. If certain jobs are eliminated due to computers replacing them, other jobs should be created to compensate.

For example, if drones were to deliver pizzas, the pizza delivery driver would be out of a job.

However, that same person could start a new career in the same field. Perhaps instead of driving a car to deliver pizza, that same person could work on building the drones, operating them, or maintaining them.

Consider the calculator. Even though a calculator might be able to do its functions at a quicker rate than many humans, there are still businesses that must sell them. The stores that sell these calculators hire employees to stock them and ring them up at the cash register. Truck drivers are also employed to deliver them, warehouse companies are established to manufacture them, and so on.

Nevertheless, machine learning is very pervasive throughout society, and although it has its limitations, it can certainly be beneficial.

www.ingramcontent.com/pod-product-compliance
Lightning Source LLC
Chambersburg PA
CBHW031231050326
40689CB00009B/1560